SITUATIONS
Life Experiences Expressed Through Poetry and Prose

Jerome Simmons

M.O.R.E. Publishers
St. Louis, MO

SITUATIONS

Life Experiences Expressed Through
Poetry and Prose

Jerome Simmons

Corrine Hines Smith, typist

ACKNOWLEGEMENT

The book is dedicated first to my lovely daughter who I hold dear in my heart. I thank God for the blessing that He bestowed upon me, when He blessed me with you. I know we have a whole lot of life that we missed together, due to my own short-comings, but we have a whole life ahead of us that we can share together, if we set aside our own stubbornness. I know I missed a lot of your special moments, as well as your personal achievements, but every moment that I spent with you was special to me.

Thank you baby, for being "not so understanding," because I needed that tough love of yours to help motivate and inspire me to rise to the occasion. If I haven't told you enough, or showed you enough, I want to set the record straight. I love you baby with all of my heart and you will forever be "Daddy's Little Girl".

To Kyenia T. Fields
A.K.A. (also known as)
Kee Kee

Thought: I can understand children
who are afraid of the dark
but it's sad to see
men who are afraid of the light!
(Author unknown)

ACKNOWLEDGEMENT

The book is also dedicated to the most wonderful woman in the world – my mother.

My mother is the one who loved me unconditionally, no matter what I took her through or went through. She was always there with support whether it was mentally, financially, or just with reasonable words.

Mrs. Simmons, I love you for many reasons because you always have done the will of God and always have let your light shine. You opened your home up to the community. Although you only had five (5) children, I believe you reared twenty-five (25) children. You worked and provided for the whole Getwell Gardens Community.

I'm sure that in every one of our lives that you encountered, you made a difference.

I just want to thank God for allowing the world to witness one of His Angels. You always put everyone before you. You did without so that others could have something.

Mrs. Simmons, all of your children and the whole community love you, and miss you.

Yes, Mom, I love you and thank you for everything because now I finally realize what you have been teaching me.

R.I.P. Yvonne Simmons
(March 29, 1947 born - April 10, 2001 died)

Dedication

Thank you, Corrine "Sweetie" Hines; for always being there pushing me every step of the way; for all the pain; and inconvenience I've caused; for all the embarrassments I've put you through.

This is for you sweetie.

May God continue to bless our love, and shed His mercy and grace upon our lives.

Love,

Jerome

_____ _____ .

Special Thanks

Special thanks, Al "Solomon" Freeman
for feeling my struggles and being a friend.

We are always "Brothers", no matter what.

Special thanks also go to my play-sister Delores Freeman.

I love you!

Situations

Life Experiences Expressed Through
Poetry and Prose

Jerome Simmons

FORWARD

This book has been too long in coming. I prolonged and procrastinated forever; but now the time has finally arrived for me to share this splendid book with the world.

These are real-life situations and never before have you heard love, reality, motivation, inspiration, A-A, special occasions, life and death expressed in this way.

The reader will automatically find their situations on numerous pages, and hopefully this book will inspire them to rise to the occasion.

Hopefully the reader will be able to rebuild broken relationships, and give thanks to God. He is the one that made it possible for you to read this book right now (March 19, 2011).

Situations

Life Experiences Expressed Through
Poetry and Prose

Jerome Simmons

INTRODUCTION

This is a different kind of book than you have read in the past because I'm a different kind of person. I've experienced life on many different walks. I've had several different situations, relating to those walks of life. So, in this book you will surely find a poem that fits your situation, or someone's situation that is near and dear to you.

The poems were written in relationship to real life experiences. No fiction is necessary, because reality itself sometimes doesn't seem real. These poems came from my heart and I'm sure they'll reach yours, especially if it's a present situation that you're going through.

Contents

Author and Sister, Melissa Simmons

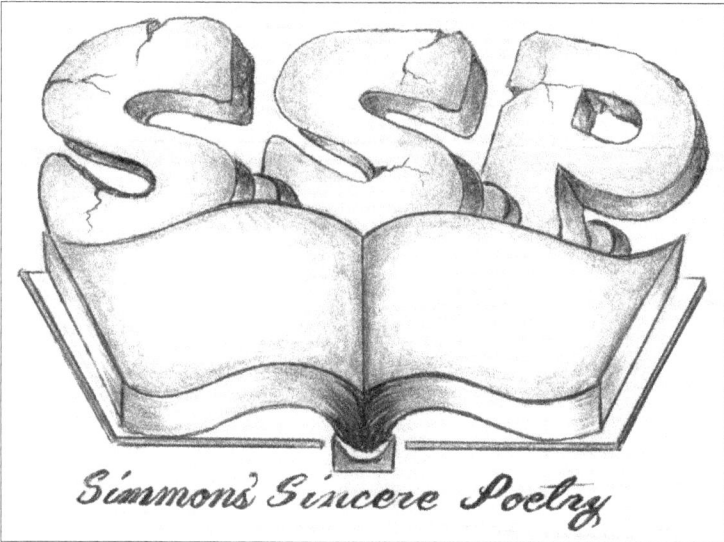

Simmon's Sincere Poetry

Artwork
by
Melvin UpChurch

ALL IN THE GAME
By Jerome Simmons

While laying across
my bunk, serving
time,

You know a whole
lot of thoughts have
crossed my mind;

About my past,
my present, and my
future, you see.
I've been enslaved all my life;
and now I am ready to be free.

I've got shackles on my feet, but they are really on my mind.
I've got to do something positive 'cause I'm constantly wasting time.
I always have been in a life of crime;
trying to get more money, but none of it was mine.

I never really had a steady job.
I use to sell dope, steal, and rob;
But now that's behind me; but my future is ahead.
I've got to straighten out my life before I end up dead.

12

The world is still moving; but I'm left behind.
I'll be a fool to try to make up for lost time.
I need a job that's what everyone's screaming and yelling;
but it's hard to find work when you've been convicted as a felon.

So I must get me some skills or better yet a trade.
Believe it or not, my bills still have to be paid.
So I'm just sitting here pouring my heart out on paper
instead of laying around plotting another caper.

I hope this writing will be my key to success.
But whether I make it or not, I still know I've been blessed.

Appreciation
By Jerome Simmons

This **Certificate** is awarded

for all you have done.

The **recognition** I'm giving

is for the honor you've won.

A short time ago when things were bad,
Peace in your heart was all you had.
Peace and nobility are all that are true.
They are covered in love for a person like you.

If generosity could be bottled and stored where it's cold
your kindness would be plentiful and worth its weight in gold.

My appreciation goes deeper than words can say,

but I hope this **Certificate**

helps brighten up your day.
This should have been said but it's also belated -
I just wanted you to know, you are appreciated.

Beautiful Black Lady
By Jerome Simmons

You're a beautiful young lady as anyone can see.
You are smart, intelligent, and kind when you want to be.
Your personality is great and so is your smile.
I just wanted to compliment you on your charm and style.

You are an independent person - now that's a plus;
and with an attitude like yours, you are easy to trust.
I want you to remain the same for the rest of your days.
Please don't let anyone change your ways.

To you my beautiful black lady with all due respect,
keep GOD in your life and you will stay in check.
Stay focused on your dreams, and pursue your goals.
Keep an opened mind and continue your role.

Don't let anyone cause you to stress,
because you are one of God's tools and this is only a test.
Just like the spinners when they sang "Sadie";
this is for you because you are a beautiful, black lady.

BROTHERS

By Jerome Simmons

I want to send this thought out to all my brothers
although we may have different fathers and mothers.
We have to stop killing and hurting one another
because when it all boils down, all we have is each other.

We need to further our education because these jobs are for real.
The Mexicans and our women have taken over the work field.

The music is still playing brothers,
but we're listening to a different song.
I just thank GOD that He made women to be our backbone.

We must admit that the women are holding the jobs and
the house down,
and too many of our brothers are on drugs, in jail, or just not around.

It's time we started standing up and being real men,
because we never know when they will notify the next of kin.

So let's start being fathers, husbands, friends, and business men.
We're behind in life and our children don't know where to begin.

So let's start right now, and do what we can
because when God made us, this wasn't in His plan.

Chance
By Jerome Simmons

There is a positive thought, to the game "Chance".
It's played with love and a little romance.
To survive this game we must use our minds,
and love each other until the end of time.

This letter of "Chance" is written especially for you.
It's to let you know what I'm going through;
for out of all my promises, there is one I kept -
after being with you, there is nothing left.

So I'm sending my love, along with this letter,
and I hope by chance that things get better.

CHANCE

If by chance, you stumble or miss a step,
I will always be there to lend a hand to help.

This letter of chance, with no time to waste,
is just a small reminder of my good taste!
For if there ever was a time for love to grow;
being apart should make it show.

So I want you to forever remember this -
whenever I'm alone, it's you that I miss.
So like a delicate perfume imported from France,
I'm sending my love in the name of "Chance".

Christmas Time

By Jerome Simmons

Christmas time comes but once a year.
That's why we should be happy, and cheer.

This is the day we celebrate Jesus' birthday.
We give thanks, give gifts, and pray.

This is the season when we share laughter and joys,
and the kids get to play with brand new toys.

Happy Birthday, Lord Jesus Christ.
We thank you for giving us new life;
And may your birthday, always be celebrated.
You came to save our soul, and we greatly appreciate it!

Confidential

By Jerome Simmons

Darling, to me, you are all I desire
when I'm feeling lonely and confused.
The way you do those things you do
to keep me loving you,
to me is confidential.

Honey, for you I would leave nothing undone.
The pledge that I make you will exceed all the limitations of joy
and still be confidential.

Sweetheart, if I had a lucky charm
or a four leaf clover, it would be you.
You are all I could wish for.
The way you apply yourself, again, to me is confidential.

Baby, your warm smile, nice looks,
and tender emotions are all dear;
but that way you have of loving
is intimately, passionately, and confidential.

Cunning, Baffling and Powerful
By Jerome Simmons

We know life is full of surprises
and that our disease comes, in many disguises.
So stop tricking yourself, like you got this thing beat,
'cause if you tempt faith, you'll find yourself back in the streets.

We know we're not stable.
We're mentally insane.
I'd hate to see you on the corner begging for change.
I know you won't go there, because you're a vet.
But we have this other thing we call "not yet"!

Today I've been delivered from that evil curse,
but if I go back to using, it can only get worse.
So I need to stay focused the best that I can,
'cause I'm sick and tired of being less than a man.

That's why I bow down and I thank my higher power above,
because I know it was Him who showed me real love.

So we need to stop thinking that everything is sourful.
That's the disease.
It's cunning. It's baffling. It's powerful!

Everyone Has a Gun
By Jerome Simmons

Everyone has a gun! Now that's a known fact.
There are more guns in the city than there are in Iraq.
They passed out these gun permits so you can protect yourself,
but things are way out of hand.
People are getting killed for theft.

Everyone has a gun in the house, or in the car.
Children are killing each other!
Now that's going way too far.

Everyone's carrying a gun like it's really cool.
Then we play stupid, when guns end up in the school.
Children only act out what they see grown-ups do.
Do you have a permit, and carry a gun too?

Facing Reality   By Jerome Simmons

I've confined myself, to a treatment center;
from using alcohol and drugs.
I had to surrender.
They have this thing called the twelve steps.
It works for those who are truly seeking help.

The information I've been given has been sound and just.
As I look over my life, I've realized I have been blessed.
As I sit around and listen to these other guys' story,
I thought I was different, but I'm in the same category.

My life is unmanageable and I have no power.
They say "One day at a time", but I'm hour by hour.
I knew I could stay sober if I just really tried
because too much of my life, I've already denied.

So I'm going to stay focused and do what's right,
because I'm struggling day to day to win this fight.
So all praise to my higher power for paving the way,
because He made it possible for me to have my sobriety today.

Forgive to Forget
By Jerome Simmons

The authority to forgive when bitterness is high
should be a balanced arrangement until the day we die.
In order to achieve with true success,
we both must learn to forgive to forget.

When two people care, the tradition should last.
It is highly recommended to forget the past.
To forgive is an advantage for us to campaign.
Remembering good times is what should remain.

For me to say, it is you to blame;
I could surely be wrong and less than a man.
I say these words. They are "forgive to forget";
for I've done this continuously since the day we met.

In my opinion we need immediate action.
So I'm sending my love with no retraction.
Forgive me darling, if this seems strong -
but if it's not necessary, then I must be wrong.

There's one thing for sure and this you can bet;
being without your love, I could never forget.
I'm sitting here wishing as I write this letter;
and hoping theses words will be a big seller.

For you, my love, the mood is set.
So from me to you, let's forgive to forget.

Good Example

By Jerome Simmons

There are trials and tribulations in every affair.
For two that care, makes a relationship rare.
A good example of how this should really go
is to skip the bad, and let the good stuff show.

Now the best thing going, that's preserved for two
is to be forgiven in everything we do.
A good example of how this should go
is to be sincere and let our feelings show.

So I'm sending this letter, in the name of good,
for my true affections should be understood.
The best example that I can give
is I'm missing you now, and always will.

If there ever was a story that was made to last,
then I hope we make it to the top of the class.
A good example took place in France.
In the name of love, Romeo took a chance.

Now, that relationship did not make it.
I will not go that far, and I will not fake it.
But what I'm trying to say, and keep it true -
a good example is that I truly miss you.

Happy Birthday

By Jerome Simmons

Another year has come and gone,
and it's a blessing to see how time moves on.
Today is your birthday so be happy and cheer,
and give thanks to God that you are still here.

Happy birthday, Baby. Today is your day.
So whatever, you should have it your way.
I know you still have a million things to do,
so whatever you attempt, may God be with you.

Sit down and rest; you're one year older.
Just for today, take the world off your shoulders.
So everybody has to listen to what you have to say,
for it's cool to shout, "IT'S MY BIRTHDAY!"

Happy Mother's Day
By Jerome Simmons

Today is Mother's Day all across the world.
Everyone can't celebrate - just the very special girls.
Everyday should be Mother's Day and not just one,
because there are not enough hours to tell what my Mom has done.

Mother, today is your day and it's all about you,
and I'm here to cater to whatever you want to do.
All year long you've been doing things to the max,
but today let me handle things; you just sit back and relax.

I thank God everyday for giving my Mom to me.
She's strong, sweet, sensitive and funny when she wants to be.
You are a good-hearted person. That really makes you a special mom.
I'd walk for miles for one of your smiles and to be held in your arms.

You're a child's fantasy and a teenager's dream,
because with a Mom like you, I'm on a winning team.
I love you mom, and may things always go your way.
I just want to make sure you have a Happy Mother's Day!

History
By Jerome Simmons

History has a way of repeating itself.
When we speak of ours, it shouldn't fall on ears that are deaf.
We have had many great people who helped paved the way.
That's how we got to where we are today.

Jackie Robinson played MLB*. He was an all-time great.
Harriet Tubman founded the Underground Railroad, which helped
slaves escape to another state.
Althea Gibson was a champion, on the tennis court;
and we now have Venus and Serena Williams holding down that sport
.

Rosa Parks remained seated on the front of the bus.
This led to the Civil Rights Movement for each of us.
Martin Luther King, Jr. led many marches and protests.
He wanted to end segregation, so that we could have the best.
We now have streets, expressways, and parks named after him,
and to learn more, you should visit the Civil Rights Museum.

Maya Angelou was a poet.
She inspired many men.
She even recited a poem during President Clinton's swearing in.
Colin Powell was the first Black to chair Joint-Chief of Staff;
and Rev Al Sharpton's voice is still crying out.
He's an activist in the civil rights movement.
It's been forty years, and a lot of improvements,

But we still have a lot of laws, which just apply to us.
So in that sense, we're still on the back of the bus.

There are a lot of people I left out,
because I couldn't mention them all,
but their names are in D. C.*, engraved on the wall.

We've had a lot of great people, that have come and I'll say "went";
but I have to mention one more – Barack H. Obama, our 44th President!

*Major League Baseball
*Washington, District of Columbus

I Love You
By Jerome Simmons

I loved you once. I loved you twice.
I love you more than dope or dice.
I do believe God above
created you, for me to love.

When I die and go up there,
I'll wait for you on a golden stair.
If you are not there by judgment day,
I'll know you went the other way.

I will give the angels back their wings,
long white robe, and other pretty things;
and just to prove my love is true,
I'll go to hell just to be with you.

I'll Be There
By Jerome Simmons

I am glad to see, that you are still in good health,
'cause if something happened to you, I wouldn't know
what to do with myself.

I just now realized how much I love you,
and how much I care.
Whatever you are going through, let me always be there.

I have known you, for only a short time,
and one thing we have is a meeting of the mind.
I hope you got your head on straight,
but if nothing else, I'm here if you want to communicate.

I Remain
By Jerome Simmons

I was young, like a cub of a wolf,
with a mind everyone seemed to overlook.
My mother has died. My father is gone.
I'm left in this world to care for my own.

Not knowing where I would go
in the rain, sleet, nor snow,.
I lived in a place where I could call home,
and for many years, I lived there alone.

I looked in the sky every night
to tell the Lord that "It just ain't right
to live my life, like a ship sailing on."
I have everything to live for.
My mother has died. My father is gone.
Yet I remain!

Keep On Keeping On
By Jerome Simmons

When we started out as friends,
I thought our relationship would never end.
We soon advanced and became lovers,
looking out and caring for one another.

Life has a way of taking its tolls,
yet I still believe, together, we can reach our goals.
We've been through good times and bad, but it's getting worse.
When you said you loved me, was that rehearsed?

You said you'd be here, in my time of need,
but some how, you found a reason to leave.
I know you need a relief, every once in a while,
and all I ever wanted was to see you smile.

But if it makes you feel good, by cutting out on me,
then I think that's the way it's supposed to be.
The blame isn't on you. The blame is on me,
because I shouldn't have been thinking so foolishly.

So you do your "thang" and remain strong,
'cause by all means, I got to keep on keeping on!

Keep Your Head Up
By Jerome Simmons

Keep your head towards the sky.
You see how fast life passes us by.
So let's take this time out to mourn and cry,
but we were all born to live and to die.

You must continue on to live your life.
You are still a sister, a daughter, a mother and a wife.
So gather your strength, for we must move on
because we never know when God's gonna call us home.

I know losing a loved one hurts real deep,
so I recommend you pray, you fast, and get you some sleep.
Be strong for your family and do what you can,
because everything that happened was part of God's plan.

Kindness
By Jerome Simmons

On this day of our Lord, with another year to show,
this certificate is awarded to a lady I know.
For as green as the grass that grows in the field,
your kindness is Rare, and Emotions are Real.

This certificate of kindness comes very high
with a touch of class that you cannot buy.
On any given day, your sensitivity will do,
and I pray to my Lord, that He watches over you.

This Certificate is awarded for the woman you are.
If I need a true friend, you're the best by far.
Admired by all, the generations of youth,
you're filled with sincerity and a symbol of truth.

For kindness to work, we must give it a try,
but for you, it is natural until the day you die.
For me it's an honor, to know a person like you.
So I'm sending this thought to see your day through.

Dating way back to the first day we met,
your kindness began, and I shall never forget.
So accept this certificate, though it carries a feeling,
from me to you, for kindness that's appealing.

Lady
By Jerome Simmons

You are a lady in every sense of the word.
You don't have to speak loud for your voice to be heard.

You are the backbone, that every man needs;
the top soil it takes to plant a good seed.

When you define lady, it spells out your name.
You are rare among women because all are not the same.

I really admire your strong sense of duty.
You get things done, without using your beauty.

You are a rich man's treasure and a poor man's wealth,
and I love the way you handle and carry yourself.

So forget all the if's, buts, and maybe's.
You are what women hope to be because you are a lady.
04/09/11

Laying it Down
By Jerome Simmons

Being involved with gangs today is really not so cool.
Have you heard the latest news?
It will get **U** kicked **outta** school.
You need a diploma, and college to make it in the world today.

I hope you remember that saying, "Crime doesn't pay!"
The jails are overcrowded with nothing but the youth.
You must have thought your elders weren't telling you the truth?

The streets ain't safe or straight.
So we need to be realistic.
Don't end up in jail, just being another statistic!

I know you don't mind working, but they paying such a small fee
but once you come to jail, you end up working for the free.
Educate yourself brother. Life ain't all that sweet.
Don't end up like the rest - shot dead in the streets!

Do something with your life. Pursue your goals or dreams.
Because don't nothing change in jail - everyday is a daily routine.

Help raise that child, and do whatever you can.
Stand up and take responsibility.
Show the world you are a real man!

I hope you young men understand what I had to say.
Life is too short, so don't throw yours away.
Start you a career and find yourself a good wife.
Don't end up like me, in and out of jail all your life!

Let Not Your Heart Be Troubled
By Jerome Simmons

Let not your heart be troubled, for we must all travel this road.
You can't do this alone, so let God carry your load.
He has a spot in your heart that will never be erased.
For now He is gone to rest in a better place.

Yet God has promised never to leave nor forsake you.
Trust in Him and hold on; God will see you through.
May God continue to strengthen you and your family.
He has not forgotten.
So when you pray, please include me.

For He truly does care.
His word states that He will be there, through all of your pain,
problems, fears and tears.
God sees all and knows all with his listening ears.
I said that, to say this, there is no situation too big or too small.
God is willing and able to cater to us all!

Life is a Breeze

By Jerome Simmons

When I wake up in the morning, and gaze at the sun,
I can recall all the days when I had my fun -
balling out of control, living life with ease,
taking penitentiary chances, thinking life was a breeze.

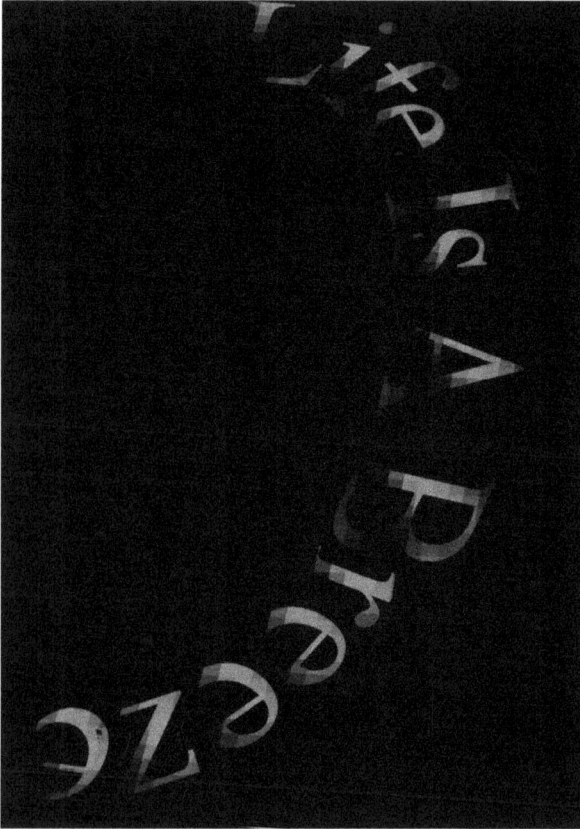

I focus on my nights and never my days, wondering why in the hell didn't I change my ways?

Now I'm going to God in prayer.

As I bow on my knees, I'm still thinking to myself, "Life is a breeze."

Lil' Bit
By Jerome Simmons

I have had this puppy since she was three months old.
She has brought happiness, joy, and peace to my soul.
She was a Christmas present I gave it to my wife.
The puppy was frisky, funny, and so full of life.

The children really enjoyed seeing her jump like a frog.
They got mad at each other for hogging the dog.
She would go hunting and bring home turtles and stuff.
I hate I didn't tell her I loved her enough.

Lil' Bit, we love you, and we hate you had to part,
but you will always have a place in each of our hearts.
We told you to quit chasing cars, but you finally got hit.
Now you are gone to doggie heaven, and we love you Lil' Bit!

Lil' Bit -
Sunrise 9-2009
Sunset 04-03-2011

Living Proof
By Jerome Simmons

During the course of romance it's easy to see
that it's not but one love in the world for me.
I thought this out carefully, to recapture truth,
when I finally realized that you're the living proof.

I don't have to know everything you do,
for it's easy to lose someone like you.
Staying together in a responsible way
is living proof that love doesn't play.

Now I know this sound just a little bit funny,
but I'm doing my best to say "I miss you, honey".
I really can't say just how I feel,
but you're living proof of what I feel is real.

And in case you're wondering just what I miss,
it's your warm embrace and passionate kiss.
Going a little deeper, like beneath the sea,
if you know what I mean, it's living proof to me.

It's really not hard to have it your way.
Just remember, my love will always stay.
Being without you is like a house with no roof.
Believe me, honey, you're my living proof.

Make it Happen

By Jerome Simmons

As I look into your eyes, there are many things I see -
all those hopes and dreams that long to be free.
Only you can make it happen.
So what are you waiting on to start?
You are still listening to your mind, instead of following your heart.

You have been holding yourself back for too many years.
It's time to apply yourself with blood, sweat, and tears.
I know you can do it, but first you gotta try.
Get off your butt and stop telling yourself that lie!

Stay focused on your dreams.
Don't let them get away.
Forget what you use to say.
Today is a new day.

We can do anything we set our minds to do.
I'm going to pursue my dreams.
What about you?
Make it Happen!

My First B-Day
By Jerome Simmons

I've been clean and sober now, for 365 days.
I know I couldn't have made it; if my higher powers hadn't changed my ways.
My thinking was shot, and my attitude was a shame.
I hung around negative people, thinking I had some "game".

Now that I've been clean for one whole year,
a whole lot of things in my life have become clear.
My life is important, and I depend on my higher power.
I enjoy being in my meetings, even if it ain't but an hour.

I now have goals, dreams, and plans that need to be fulfilled.
They can only become possible, if it's my higher power's will.
I've surrounded myself around positive people and things,
and I can't describe the happiness that sobriety brings.

I just want to thank my higher power, for delivering me.
Now I know how to live happily, joyously, and free.
So special thanks to the program, for paving the way,
and I thank each of you, for celebrating my first Birthday!!

My Sweetie
By Jerome Simmons

I asked this young lady to be my wife.
I promised to love, honor, and cherish her for life.
We've had bad times, hard times, and it's still kind of tough,
but she doesn't worry about materials things.
She says my love is enough.

I constantly found ways to leave her side -
chasing money and material things because of my pride.
She tells me to sit myself down; everything's going to be alright.
But doing my struggles, I feel I've lost another fight.

But now I put everything in God's hand
because whatever I can't do, I know that He can.
I asked God to forgive me, and now I'm asking you.
I just want to see you happy, because you know my love is true.

This is for you my love; no one else will do.
It's kind of rough right now, but I know you'll see me through.
So let's end this war, and sign us a treaty,
because my future would be nothing without you, my sweetie!
3/16/2011

Never Afraid

By Jerome Simmons

When I was growing up as a child,
I hung with a group of boys, and all of us were wild.
People were scared of us, so I thought I had it made;
and when real trouble came I was never afraid.

As I grew into a teen, I committed a crime.
I landed in juvenile, for my very first time.
The officers told me, "This could lead you to your grave".
That was music to my ears because I wasn't afraid.

As I entered manhood, I did many things.
I wasn't scared, so I could handle anything.
The first time I got scared is when I heard God's voice.
I only heard it once, so I continued to make my choice.

As I grew older and started living my life,
I tried my hand at love, not once but twice.
I gave God my attention, and my lady my best.
That's when I realized, I was afraid of success!
3/16/2011

One More Hurt
By Jerome Simmons

I have been using drugs, and doing time, for the last twenty years.
I've caused bloodshed, heartaches, and my family many tears.
I realize each and every one of us was born with a soul
and there's only one way to go through life - either in or out of control.

I've had some dry times, many times in the past,
but like everything else in my life, that too didn't last.
I can recall anticipating using alcohol and drugs.
That was my substitute for all those kisses and hugs.

I use to shine big time while doing my thing
for I wasn't thinking about the heartaches, the disappointments, and
the pain it would bring.
Running like a mad man, doing whatever it took;
I woke up one day in jail, and realized I had become a crook.

So I entered the program to get my life on track,
but after a few months the streets called, and you know I went back.
I used a couple of times and quit because the high just wasn't the
same.
What really got me was that I got caught up in the game.

I started back hustling, swanging, and giving people hell.
I hit my bottom when I lost everything, and went back to jail.
Although I was clean at the time, I thought I had an advantage in the
game,
but I didn't change my lifestyle, and the results were still the same.

Our Neighborhood
By Jerome Simmons

We have to start taking pride in our community.
But first, we need to have some peace and unity.
We're killing each other at a rapid pace.
Why can't we get along, with our own black race?

We're using drugs, toting guns, and still gang banging.
Brothers are walking the hood with their pants hanging.
On every other corner, you see a brother swanging.
But we are forgetting these women and children that we left hanging.

I pray to God that these organizations and gangs come together
because this way of living has got to get better.
The elderly people are afraid to come out the door,
because it's not safe to walk the neighborhood any more.

There is too much corruption and hate in our neighborhood.
It's time we come together, and turn bad into good.
So let's make our community and streets safe again.
We can start by coming together
being brothers, friends, and real men!

Perilous Times
By Jerome Simmons

We're living in some perilous times,
where people are committing all sorts of crimes:
home invasions, robbery, carjacking and theft.
It seems that no one even cares about themselves.

Every time I see the news, it talks about a homicide.
Whatever happened to the people and their self-pride?
I just read about all the crooked cops,
and I asked myself "When and where does this stop?"

The politicians are crooked, and won't pay their bills.
Then we got those who are making all kinds of side deals.
The president has sent hundreds of thousands to war,
and after they got killed, he asked to send more.

We've got homeless people fending for their meals,
and half the country is strung out on pills.
We're living in some perilous times'
where people are educating, and corrupting our minds.

Too many senseless killings are going on today.
I ask the world to come together, and let's all bow and pray.

We already have people living on the moon,
so we need to prepare ourselves because God is coming for us soon!

Quorum

By Jerome Simmons

In the beginning it was just us two.
We got together for something to do.
We made up our minds to be together -
loving, caring, always, and forever.

We added the bad, but it's coming out good.
So I want you to know that I understood
that every thing we said was for the best,
and we made it through, without the rest.

Quorum means down to you and me.
which is the smallest number for things to be.
We'll make mistakes, but let's not stop.
Let's keep it together and open up shop.

The sooner the better, it's never too late.
If it's for us together, I just can't wait to end this Quorum.
We are the store.
For you and me it's gonna be some more, and some more.

Reality
By Jerome Simmons

I've found myself in a detrimental situation once again -
calling on God; He's my only friend.

I've made many bad choices, throughout my life;
hurting myself and everyone else, that was involved in my strife.

I relied on self-will 'cause I thought I could do it all.
That was my biggest mistake and it caused me to fall.

I can't do anything without the help of God.
If you haven't found Him, now Is the time for you to start!

Recognition
By Jerome Simmons

Out of all the things, in the world to do,
what I need the most is to be with you.
Like a beautiful goddess, and just the right size,
your technique is simple, and has been recognized.

And out of all the colors, in the world to see,
recognizing your passion is enough for me.
For me to see you in a lonely situation
makes me realize you are too much temptation.

Recognition is yours for being so sweet.
Your charm and style are what I'd like to meet.
If I ever get tricked on the same ole thang,
just thinking of you, could bring about a change.

Audacious am I, both daring and bold,
for the way you make me feel will not be told.
It's really not a secret and surely not a petition.
so I'm taking this time to send you recognition.

When life seems dull, there's only one thing to do -
take all my inner feelings and direct them to you.
For all those little things, we seem to forget,
I now give recognition, dating back to when we met.

So don't let this poem come as a surprise.
I want you to know, you've been Recognized.

Redd Hott
By Jerome Simmons

There's a feeling in the air and it's going around.
When it's cold outside, it can heat the ground.
Like the angels of love, who only needs one shot,
when I think of you, the thought is redd hott!

It's a feeling of warmth, truth, passion and fear.
I had the same one when we met my dear.
Impatient I may be, but crazy I'm not.
Just the thought of you gets me redd hott!

You know a true sense of love can change one's mind.
But with a lady like you, it gets better with time.
Isolated by affections, when there's little to do,
is a redd hott feeling all the way through!

So excuse me darling, for putting us on the spot,
but I'm sending my love, and it's coming redd hott!

Remembrance

By Jerome Simmons

As I wake up each morning, and gaze at the sun,
I recall all the days when we had our fun.

Two fools in love or so it seemed,
but now that I'm awake,
I realize it was all a dream.

I still think back to the day we met.
Now that's one day I will never forget.
As I looked out my window, I saw two butterflies land -
one on a rock, and the other on some sand.

I thought to myself "What are they gonna do?"
Then I realized it was me feeling blue.

Serious Business

By Jerome Simmons

To a very serious lady from a serious man -
I will try to be as honest the best that I can.
From a man like me with charm and finesse -
my profound idea is some serious business.

So if a million dollars is what you need,
work hard at your goal and save indeed.
If the perfect guy is what it takes,
then I'll be your prince and not your snake.

I'm serious-minded and business at heart.
My ability to achieve needs no other part.
When it comes to life I cannot lose.
Seriously speaking, replacing "B.S." I'll choose.

In running a business it's like having a rash.
The affection can spread so keep plenty of cash.
Thinking out loud, my business with you
is one way to succeed and this we can do.

Talking like a gentleman, the "B.S." can go.
What I can do for you, I'll have to show.
But back to the beginning in the garden of Eve,
they say Eve was put there for Adam's needs.
But as it may, we can pass the test
if we keep our minds on some serious business.

Sincere
By Jerome Simmons

To a very sincere lady, and a close personal friend,
this certificate is awarded, for the way you have been.
To be handled with care, when my mind is clear,
you're all I need and I'm being sincere.

Sincerity is an emotion that can surely stand alone.
It keeps me settled whenever you are gone.
If I should fall asleep when there's little to do,
you can rest assured, I am thinking of you.

There's nothing in this world, and I say this with care,
can come between our love, and this I swear.
I sincerely hope without any delay,
that the feelings we share will always stay!

An additional thought, when the others are lost,
is I'm here to please, no matter what the cost.
For you my love, I would do my very best,
to express my ideas and let sincere do the rest.

For to be sincere we must be for real,
cut out the games, and be honest, better still.
If ever in doubt and love plays a part,
experience helps, but rely on your heart!

Special Occasions
By Jerome Simmons

On special occasions I'll have you to know
that my thoughts of you will always show.
My wish for you on any special day is to be wanted, and needed, the
fashionable way.

Special

Occasion

And if that doesn't work, especially for you,
then I hope all your wishes and dreams come true.
For no matter how far, or no matter how long it shall take,
I'll be both your feeling and icing on the cake!

So on special days, when I'm not there,
believe me honey, I truly do care!

Stop Wasting Time

By Jerome Simmons

Brothers and sisters, we have to stop wasting time.
Instead of saying everything is alright, we need to educate our minds.
We have to reach out to one another and lend that helping hand,
because divided we fall, but united we stand!

As I sit around and analyze the clock,
I recall they use to have both a tick and a tock.
Now they just have a tick. I guess the tock wasn't steady,
but what we fail to realize is we're missing a beat already!

Brothers and sisters, we have to stop wasting time.
They are proposing to build a brand new jail and you know who they
got in mind.
We need to talk to our loved ones and then talk to strangers,
because at the rate things are going, our race is in danger!

It's hard to reproduce when we're in jail or on drugs,
and what our children really need are education, love, and hugs.
They need real men around, to really show them the way.
We can't wait on tomorrow.   We have to show them today!

So let's start right now by utilizing our minds.
Brothers and sisters, we got to stop wasting time!

Thank God
By Jerome Simmons

When I wake up in the morning, before my feet hit the floor,
I thank God for today, and pray for many more.
The first thing I do, is read me a verse,
'cause I remember the times when I use to do worse.

I now get my pleasure, out of pleasing the Lord.
That's how I know that everything else is void.
I thank God each day for my health and strength.
To stay focused on God, I go to any length.

God is good, and He always has been.
Let's share that thought with our family and friends.
He has this mercy, and grace that He gives.
All He asked us to-do, was give up our self-will.

Let's put our trust in Him, and let Him lead the way.
Every time I run my life, I end up going astray!

The Past
By Jerome Simmons

Just looking back at the past;
seeing a life, that would never last;
remembering the things that I use to do,
and remembering, I use to like them too.

Breaking, entering, and robbing too,
those are just a few things, that I use to do.
Breaking people's hearts was just a part.
Even taking people through a lot of pain - I must have been
going insane.

Stealing as the days would come and go,
I thought I was fast, but I was really slow.
I didn't have anyone to blame.
I just was out there, doing my thang.

Always putting value on material things;
never realizing the pain it brings;
Finally I got tired of running from town to town,
and I thank God, I'm still above ground.

Thinking of all the things that I have done wrong,
living a fast life, isn't going to last long.
I never had a reason why.
Just thinking about it, makes me cry.

All the things that I've done, I do regret;
and my past, I do want to forget.

THE TRUTH
By Jerome Simmons

As I blend my faith upon the hands of GOD,
I want to be saved, and I know where to start.
As sin enters my life everyday,
I know I have to bow down to God and pray.

I ask God to forgive me of all my sins,
and I pray for my family, my loved ones, my enemies and friends.
I pray for all the children who are caught up in our mess,
and I pray for all of those who have not yet confessed.

I ask Him to continue to shed His mercy and grace upon us,
and to hold us safely in His hands from the cradle to the dust.
I thank Him for the blessings that only He can give,
and I thank Him for allowing me to do his will.

I don't think I'm saved, but someday I will be.
I just want to live my life constantly depending upon Thee.
He's Lord over the world, and king of the universe.
That's why in my life, I've learned to put Him first!

Thinking of You
By Jerome Simmons

Traveling about is sometimes strange on the crowded highways and
dusty range.
When I'm feeling moody, as I sometimes do,
it's an appropriate moment for thinking of you.

My love is a highway stretching from me to you,
with no overpass, no bypass, no pit-stops to do.
You may enter at will. The speed limit is slow.
There are no known exits, with only one direction to go.

Energy and an opened heart are all you will need,
for my highway of love is a long one indeed.
You may follow the signs of the stars above
and bring nothing but your heart to find my love.

My highway of love, with no twists or turns,
is directed at you with a passion that burns.
So on these restless nights, with feelings of blue,
The nights come out sunny, when I think of you.

So follow the path of a misty dove
and enter at will, my highway of love.
The time is right. So see me through,
and remember always, I am thinking of you!

TRUE MAC
By Jerome Simmons

There's a known fact that has come to pass.
A Mac's roll will always last.
No matter what they say, no matter how true,
one thing for sure is I truly need you.

A bonafide Mac knows just what he needs.
When it comes to money, he is there to please.
To all who holds it, he serves with grace,
for he never fails to win a race.

The ways of a Mac is that he rolls twenty-four hours.
While asleep in bed, he is soaking up powers.
Cautious, and kind, but willing to fight,
when he's with the right lady, it's truly a sight.

So from me to you, with tender loving care,
you can be my lady, if you so dare.
I'll make you a pledge, which will last to the end,
to be a sympathetic lover, and a compassionate friend.

VALENTINE'S DAY
By Jerome Simmons

Here's a thought that I would like to make clear,
and that's Valentine's Day comes but once a year.
It's a day that "lovers share cards, gifts, and/or maybe a teddy bear"!

I don't have any of that, not even a rose,
but I can say I love you; and that God knows.
So keep me in your heart, because you'll always be in mine,
but I have to ask this question, "Will you be my valentine?"

Wake Up Men
By Jerome Simmons

It's time to wake up and see what's really going on.
Why we don't have enough men left in our homes?
Our women are raising the children alone.
What happened to the men? Are they all dead and gone?

To you, young men, who are affiliated, or in a gang today,
society doesn't accept that, so we must choose another way.
We're focused too much on clothes and transportation.
We need to focus more on getting an education!

Wake up men! What's really going on?
The government is providing houses.
That's one reason we can't go home.
We need to come together, push and pull,
because dealing with this young generation,
our hands are gonna be full.

We need to do all we can to get them straight;
but first we must learn to communicate.
So let's take this to the streets, and quit passing the buck,
because if we don't do something now,
We're gonna self-DE-struck!

What the Program Suggests
By Jerome Simmons

Get with the program if you want to live.
What got you in this position was your own self-will.
So keep your mouth closed because you know too much.
In order for this to work, you got to dummy up.

This program is simple. It's not designed to be hard.
Einstein couldn't get this, because he's way too smart.
It took a clown like Bozo who had little to say.
That's the reason why he's clean and sober today!

It doesn't matter if you're poor, or have plenty of wealth.
The program is here to love you until you can love yourself.
You don't know anything. I want to make that clear,
because your best thinking is what got you here!

You got to be willing to go to any length, and do whatever it takes.
You can sit around, laugh and joke, but it's your life that's at stake.
The program will only work if you're truly seeking the help.
It's been tried and tested already.
It's called the 12 steps.

You need to find you a sponsor. There are still some good ones left,
because as the program suggests "It's a fool who sponsors himself".
You know a few of us make it, out of every class,
but if you work these steps throughly, all of us will last.

So get with the program. If you want to live.
Bow down to your higher power and give up your self-will!

Where Do We Go From Here?
By Jerome Simmons

I started writing this poem, with you on my mind.
A person like you is so hard to find.
You are truly beautiful, inside and out.
You have a sweet personality, without a doubt.

The way you express yourself is crystal clear,
and I'm still wondering, where do we go from here?
Let's take a vacation, visit every state,
and without using words, let's communicate.

Conclusion

By Jerome Simmons

A preliminary fact that I want you to know
is I'm not Casanova and I don't know Romeo.
If my conversation fades, I blame none but myself.
With a lady like you, there's only one conclusion left.

Either I'm very fortunate, or motivated by mind.
My recommendation is love; but my enemy is time.
I'm not trying to trick you, but this is all I can do.
I'm just a sentimental fellow, and the drama is "you"!

My final conclusion, eliminating love and sex
is the traditional days, when the truth was next.
In case your curiosity isn't quite satisfied,
my fullest cooperation is confirmed on the ride.

It is easy to distinguish between now and the past.
The motivation is gone, and the present doesn't last.
If I had to conclude in a legitimate way,
I would shift my emotions and practice all day.

Insignificant or not, I would do all I could
to control your desires if you think I should.
My maximum romance and love in reserve
are surely complex and waiting for the word.

In concluding this letter your love will do.
I'm waiting for the answer - my choice is you.

Ladies In My Life
By Jerome Simmons

This is for the ladies in my life:
My mom, my daughter, my sister, my wife.
These are the people who kept me afloat
when I was out in the water, without a boat.

My Mom held it down, for so many years,
and my daughter - I cost her too many tears.
My sister - she's always picked up the slack.
God blessed me with Sweetie; now she's got my back.

These are the women I hold near and dear,
and I wish that Mrs. Simmons was still here.
But she's gone home to her resting place,
but when I look at Melissa, I still see Mom's face.

I thank God for the ladies in my life:
my Mom, my daughter, my sister, my wife.

Acknowledgments

This is for my first love Karen A Graham (A.K.A. Goodie); Michelle Bradford (Lil Pimpin); Lillian McKay (Gott); Sandra Brown (Bad girl); Home Girls: Sharon Oliver, Sharon Hall, Nicole, Celeste Peterson, Michelle Beason (R.I.P.), Tiny, and Rita; Rang-o-tang, my guy, through it all you are truly a friend. When it was cold outside, and I had no one to turn to, you were there. When it was hot and I needed shade, you were there. And although we don't talk too often, and we haven't spoken on this yet, I know if I need a friend, you'll be there. To the rest of "State Pen"

To all of our mothers who had a hand in raising us "hard heads" - THANKS! Richard B-Man; Ralph, Kenny Davis; Kenny Malone; Papose (Papoose); Richard Collins; Darrell Walker (R.I.P.); Lil' Charlie; L.V.; Ricky Suell; Greg Hall; Ray Taylor; Peanut; The Junior "State Pen" and all my real gangstas that I mentored and who mentored me over the years. I can truly say that I taught a lot only because I learned a lot from each of you. May you all keep me in your prayers, because that's how I made it to give thanks today - only on prayers;

To Angelee, a real gift from God who just inspire and motivate, and bring out the best in people. Thank you for working with me hands on, and inspiring me to rise to the occasion. This book has been too long in coming; only because of my own short comings, and procrastination, after procrastination. This book is dedicated to the countless people that I've encountered, along the road of truth. I always have believed that God put people and things in your life, at different times for different reasons, and confirmations. So I would like to give all my thanks to God, for putting these words in my heart, and allowing me to put them on paper.

My greatest thanks go out to my mother Yvonne Simmons. I also want to acknowledge my father Morris Simmons for being the man he is, although we didn't spend much time together, I still love ya' Pop.

I want to give special thanks to my sister Melissa for always being there regardless of how much trouble I've caused her and the inconvenience she's been through dealing with me. Yet thanks "Sweetie" for never giving up on me.

To Eric, Brenda, Rodney, Denise, Flap, may he rest in peace (R.I.P.); and to all my friends, Getwell Gardens, Walter Simmons, all my Real G's; to everyone who believed in me, and disagreed with me. Thank you all for making it happen. If I forget to mention anyone, you know who you are that made a difference in my life.

Words of Wisdom

Keep your thoughts positive, because your thoughts become your words.
Keep your words positive, because your words become your actions.
Keep your actions positive, because your actions become your habits.
Keep your habits positive, because your habits become your lifestyle.
Keep your lifestyle positive, because your lifestyle becomes your Destiny.
(author unknown)

Words of Wisdom
(To: Mrs. Special)

It's better to lose your pride to the one you love, than to lose the one you love because of pride... (author unknown)

SITUATIONS

Life Experiences Expressed Through
Poetry and Prose

Fiancees Jerome Simmons and Corrine Hines

Prepare yourself to be inspired and uplifted, with my spiritual poems, and motivational poems.

Break out those handkerchiefs for those reality poems because we have mixed emotions when reality really sets in.

Read and enjoy the relationship poems, and recommend to all of your friends that "This is a must have book and everyone should own their own personal copy."

Jerome Simmons
March 17, 2011

Cover Art by Melvin UpChurch
Printed in the United States of America
©2011

www.ingramcontent.com/pod-product-compliance
Lightning Source LLC
Chambersburg PA
CBHW060159070426
42447CB00033B/2227